Bohemian Love

Dedicated to

All the broken-hearted Girls

Also by Catherine Vaughan

The Quarter Life Crisis Poet

Welcome to Wonderland

About the Author

Catherine Vaughan is an English Writer. She has performed poetry at The Times and The Sunday Times Cheltenham Literary festival and featured in Hay Festival's Talking about Shakespeare series. The Quarter Life Crisis Poet is her debut poetry book. Welcome to Wonderland is her first novel.

Bohemian Love

Copyright © 2021 Catherine Vaughan

Published in the United Kingdom by Nova Writ Press.
www.CatherineVaughan.com

The right of Catherine Vaughan to be identified as the author of this work has been asserted in accordance the Copyright, Designs and Patents Act of 1988

All rights reserved. No part of this book may be reproduced by any mechanical, photographic, or electronic process, or in the form of a phonographic recording, nor may it be stored in a retrieval system, transmitted, or otherwise be copied for public or private use- other than for "fair use" as brief quotations embodied in articles and reviews without prior written permission of the publisher.

Bohemian Love

CATHERINE VAUGHAN

CONTENTS

I THE LOUVRE

In the Louvre   19

II DAYS BEFORE I MET YOU...

Paris Runway   22

Həʊˈtel   24

Artists on the Left bank   26

An Artist finds his Muse...   28

III DREAM WITHIN A DREAM...

The Courtship   36

The Rules   38

Champagne breakfast at The Savoy   39

IV EVERYTHING WAS GOING PERFECTLY UNTIL MY EX ARRIVED....

Mr. E. Corrival   42

Back here   44

The Second Meeting   46

V POET'S LIFE

Life of a Poet   48

Other days   51

VI BACK TO YOU

London, Paris, away…   53

Family affair   55

Frames   56

Loving you   57

Letters   58

Peonies on my doorstep   71

With you   63

Fontaine des Mers   65

VII BOHEMIA LIVES

Princess of Bohemia   68

Bohemian Royalty   71

Velvet Haze   74

VIII   THE LOVES BEFORE YOU…

Last Summer	76
The Guitar	78
By the Lake	79

IX   PASSIONS

The Fall	82
Deep / the depths of her soul	83
Ethereal / Ephemeral	84
Bohemian Love	89

X   THE SADNESS WE ALL HIDE…

Powder room	91
By and Bye	94
Lonesome	95
The Notebook on the mantlepiece	96
Crown of tears	99
Reflection	100

XI ONE DARK NIGHT WITH YOU

Volition 107

XII LOVE DESTROYS

Maybe love isn't what we think it is 114

Looking out onto the garden 118

When I Look At Her 119

This way to love/Roadblock to love 120

XIII WAKING UP WITH A BROKEN HEART…

I Will Remember You 121

Everything I never told you 122

When he fell to his knees 123

The Hermès scarf you left me 125

Pale blue shirt lullaby 126

The Waves 128

Forgive me, forgive me 129

When we met 130

Loves Trivium 131

The Balcony	135

XIV GIRL IN THE MIRROR

Portrait de Femme	139

XV INSIDE THE LIVES OF BEAUTIFUL PEOPLE

Sweet Clover	144
Little Miss Envied	146
Woven girl in denim pinafore.	148
My Valentine	152
Emerald eyes, Gypsy heart	155
Prince Albero	159
The Poet	161

XVI LITTLE TEARS

THE END

Once upon a Wonderland	195

I The Louvre

In the Louvre

You are gazing at my favourite
painting. I stand back and wait.

A girl walks to you.
My eyes cast down.

Distracting myself
I search for a sculpture.

When I find it, I am tempted to touch the white
marble: an embrace by cupid.

Secretly, I wish to be kissed the same way.
It has been so long…

That evening, at the Eiffel tower
I see you again, you hold our gaze.

Sensing recognition
Recalling the girl by your side

I look away to devour the city lights.
The night sky is arrogant with beauty.

On the hour illumination and sparkles
shine on all igniting rapture.

You walk towards me
I assume you'll go past.

You say hello
and recount seeing me in the Louvre.

I'm taken aback. My breath deepens,
I hold onto the railing.

She was only his sister,
she lives here.

I take quiet delight in what he says.
He wants to meet for breakfast,

I gently decline saying that I am
en route to Giverny.

He is persistent. And so, we agree to
visit theMusée de l'Orangerie the day after.

Thursday arrives though I am not sure he will.
An hour later and we are gazing at a painting,

The Water Lilies: Green reflections inside the
museum. Though we are in Paris, you tell me of

your travels how you saw Caravaggio in
Valletta and Guernica in Madrid.

He wants to hold hands
instead, I hold tightly to my handbag.

I return to England soon
we are really only three hours away.

Deep down I am testing him because it all
seems too good to be true.

Weeks later I am home filled with wonder
and delight at what is unfolding…

II   Days before I met you…

Paris Runway

I went to Paris to run away. A weekend, alone
to look at art, to find myself, escape everything
be a new person for a few days.

Before, I wanted to go to Paris to fall in love.
I wished and longed for this for so long and on
trips before was always disappointed.

Sitting alone in restaurants, wishing a handsome
stranger would come by
and sweep me off my feet.

I wondered if I would ever hold hands with a
guy as I walked the streets of Paris. I just
wanted someone to make memories with.

Then, this spring I went for calm
to escape the chaos of home
I didn't need to run to a man.

I needed to visit the Palace Vendôme. In the
early evening I walked past The Ritz to see a
lady step out in Haute Couture.

I took it as a sign that she would be all that I
would become. I took self-portraits on my
phone with my favourite paintings.

Paintings created by the world's greatest artists.
How can a man compare to that? There are so
many quaint cafes to explore,

scenery to draw as I nibble on petit fours
I didn't need to fall in love this time
as I was already deeply in love with life

and all the magic of Paris.

Həʊˈtel

My Louis Vuitton luggage is rugged as I
excitedly get out my precious dresses and
jewellery. I have been saving my best dresses

for this trip. These garments have waited years
to be worn and are faintly whispering gratitude
as they are delighted to be in the City of Lights

Holding them upon my body, I listen as they
tell me which museums they want to attend my
Paris street style is almost ethereal

pale pink and paler greens echo through my
ensemble. I find myself popping back to the
hotel morning, afternoon and evening so I can

wear a new dress for each new place. Not that I
brought many clothes with me I simply *bought*
more. The hotel lobby stands warmly

welcoming guests and bidding farewell in
minutes. Inside Galeries Lafayette I catch my
reflection and see my Cheeks cerise.

Lipstick fading from all the treats of Angelina

Paris. Hair teased wildly from hurriedly
walking to and from cafes, museums the metro

and back again. After walking through the
Jardin des Tuileries, I take delight in my French
soles keeping their elegance after all these hours

Alone at night I slip into a silk robe, the colour
of morning champagne. I look in the mirror one
last time knowing that tomorrow I have to

return back home, to the chaos of my life
This whirlwind of charm is coming to an end
but I know I can always come back, and maybe

next time with the man I love.
For Paris is a place where dreams come true,
and life becomes magic and ethereal…

Artists on the Left Bank

I walk alone
along the same path as Matisse.

Near the river I find a bench and sit reading
Colette, lost with Claudine.

In my hand is a little gift bag
I could not resist earlier buying yet another

silk slip dress and robe
I am so charmed by the boutiques and tried on

so many dresses yesterday guiltily buying more
that, I do not need.

Earlier I picked up a painting from a street
artist. There are cute guys on vespas and

dashing waiters. Inside my handbag sits a
notebook of scribblings of exhibitions,

restaurants, and the number of my hotel. I'm a
little old-fashioned like that.

I even have a plain papered notebook and
pencils so I can draw when the mood inspires.

I find a beautiful café and sit prettily with my
Almond croissant and coffee

Parisian landmarks in the distance
I attempt to sketch all that I see

and it's a unique blur of people, places and
fine details upon the cream pages

Bohemian pretensions
are betrayed as I

tiptoe to Hermès
gifting myself a scarf.

I walk out with my hair down, fiddling to tie my
hair into a low side ponytail with my new silk
scarf.

Inside I am longing to stay at a Palatial hotel…
By the end of the afternoon, I am walking along

the Pont Alexandre III and the gilded statues
emits the last glow of gold before the night
comes.

An Artist finds his Muse…

A widow stays at The Ritz alone, again. She has experienced all that life has to offer except true love.

Her love was taken too soon to sire a family. Yet she is young in spirit and desired by young men.

Throughout her stay this young man is like a shadow, dutifully nearby whenever she needs anything.

Our attendant is handsome, a struggling Artist. He watches her as she sits alone night after night.

Each day he takes in her beauty and at night draws her face. He longed to take her to the Left Bank

Little did he know she longed to escape her life and live as the people did, cycling to places, going on long walks at night.

It did not matter that she was older, he knew she needed to be loved to be held, listened to and cherished

she had everything but love. That love was
following her like a shadow, unbeknownst
across the hall at breakfast

he stands, waiting for his moment he was the
type of man she dreamed about in her youth
but could never be with

due to societal expectations. On a warm
afternoon through the car window, she sees
children eating ice cream and travelling students

picking up trinkets for loved ones back home.
She has had the best of everything and yet
nothing, no love, no companionship

just closets of Hermès to come home to. Having
everything people wished for she joked a Birkin
can't love you back.

Wealth occluded her hearts desires. That night
he won a bet and swapped uniforms with the
doorman he waited for his lady

and as she walked out for dinner he offered his
hand to help her down the steps and at

last she looked into his eyes.

They stood in front of each other her hand in his. "It's still early, would you join me?" She asked.

He took his hat off and went into the car sitting in the back with her, at last, she confessed she remembered seeing him.

He assumed she never noticed that all uniformed staff look the same. "Where do you like to eat?"
He mumbled a place.
"Ok, take me there."
The car stopped, not far from the hotel

and they both got out heading to the nearest menswear store where she picked out his outfit. After charging it on her card the attendant went

into the changing rooms and put on the clothes. Then they headed into an elegant boutique and she slipped out of her evening dress into more

smart-casual attire. The driver took the young man's borrowed uniform and her designer dress and the two of them headed into the streets of

Paris.

They walked back to his apartment and hopped on his vespa, her dress rising up a little as she sat on the back.

They arrived at a Lebanese restaurant family owned his Uncle treated them to anything they wanted.

Upon the rooftop they looked onto the Paris skyline, no landmarks just Parian streets and building blocks of commerce.

He enveloped her in a leftover shawl and wanted to kiss her. Though she is reserved he can't resist inviting her to his place, and she accepts.

As he looks in the kitchen for something to drink, she walks to his desk and sees a sketchbook left open. A beautiful lady's side

profile is etched on the pages. Her eyes light up in recognition. It is her. There were other paintings of his on the walls and when he

returned from the kitchen, he mentioned his

nights spent painting until the early hours. The widow stands at the window balcony and the

artist comes and put his arms around her from behind. Looking back at him reminds her of the engagement night with her late husband

He was gone too soon. When he was alive, he was always away on business, so it was hard to tell if whispers that their union

was more of a merger than a marriage had any truth to it. It was late and she knew it was time to end it. The driver had been called and was

sitting mystified outside the apartment. "I'm leaving in a couple of days, I guess I'll see you at the hotel."

But she never did.
That romantic encounter cost him his job. A couple weeks later from her upper east side

apartment she calls his gallery, requesting a commission: a portrait of a lady he spent the night with on a rooftop.

When the gallery speaks to our artist, he's a little embarrassed as his paintings are of landscapes, so a portrait request seems unusual,

perhaps she had seen his sketchbook? Was this even the same person, maybe someone got the artists name mixed up?

Pride almost got the better of him but the money was too tempting, so he agreed. The gallery was astounded she was offering thrice

the price of portraits. It was a good three months until the portrait painting was completed. At the gallery he managed to find

the commissioner's Paris address, *was it she?* A month later he knocked on the door, but nobody answered.

A week later he tried again, this time with a letter in his hand. The letter expressed gratitude and a fond recollection of their time together, he

admitted he had not stop thinking about her and wanted to see her again, so left an address. Later that year she arrived back to her Paris

home and made a surprise visit. A young girl opened the door, no doubt his girlfriend she thought. She did not know who he was. Her

boyfriend came up to the door and recognised
the name explaining he moved out. There was
only the gallery left, a rude receptionist picked

up the phone explaining the artists details could
not be disclosed. As she walked the streets
alone, she thought back to their night together,

wishing she let him kiss her if that was their last
chance together. Then she thought about the
Lebanese restaurant so went back and sipped on

a sparkling rose drink. The uncle was not in
sight, up in the rooftop the scent of the night
mystically returned.

Being together would ignite a cultural clash
they were already from such different worlds.
She was old enough to know better.

It was getting late, families and friends were
filling the tables of the restaurant, she looked on
wishing to sit amongst them and be a part of

something, wanting to belong.

As she stepped out

                    he walked in

rushing, late for his shift.
His uncle already disapproving
But there she was again

he reached out for her hand
and it was like their first meeting
this time with rose water, lemons and fenugreek

filling the air he gave her hand a kiss he did not
walk out with her instead invited her in

                    and this time she stayed.

III   Dream within a Dream…

The Courtship

He was an art school dropout who went on to study and work in finance.

Charming me with tales of his travels sailing in the French Riviera, pearl diving in Bahrain

and playing polo in Argentina.
I sat in awe.

His mother French, father English. I could not believe he was Catholic.

Gifting me with a new dress every time we went out.

Wine tasting, gourmet coffees. A painting class, afternoon tea at Fortnums.

Occasional fine dining. My life felt like a dream…

Whirlwind, life, love, money, politics, religion… We spoke about everything.

Some weekends he'd pop to Paris to see family,
he invited me, but I did not want to

rush anything. I did not want to wake up from
this. How long could it really last?

The Rules

And so, it begins…
he promised to see me again in three weeks.

He's actually based in London 3 hours away
but visiting family for the summer.

He starts a new job September
so we will both be on British soil.

The promise: correspond only by
handwritten letters.

Numbers exchanged
weekly calls at the weekend.

No texting:
except for scheduling.

Jean-Pierre's surname
is unknown.

Never 2 weeks without seeing each other from
September onwards.

Champagne breakfast at The Savoy

A breakfast banquet at 2am
from room service earlier
ordering what we please

Decadence dancing
in front of mirrors
recreating moves
from the party

Sunrise
across the Thames
last sip of champagne

Finally, falling asleep…
Lunchtime comes…

Shopping in Covent garden
Ladurée macarons
Rose petal, orange blossom, pistachio
sitting pretty

Hop to Harrods,
Hands reach for Van Cleef & Arpels
You try on watches
as I trace my fingertips across necklaces
only you can afford.

Harvey Nicks
I pose in dresses
made for garden parties
You kissing me
endlessly
in the dressing room.

Outside
Aveline green
silk dress
for me
another gift from you
as we
walk to
Hyde Park

Picnic with
Food hall finds
Pashmina scarf
sits on the grass
Portrait mode
iPhone
he leans in
holding me in the park
tagging me online

He reaches for my

French pastry
I playfully steal it back

He conquers as usual.

Sunday tomorrow
another magical day
with you.

Before you set off,
again without me.

IV   Everything was going perfectly until my ex arrived….

Mr. E. Corrival

Upon my happiness
he enters
uninvited.

Again.
Shadow of perpetual doubt
and tribulation.

Cold, calculating
playing a game only he understands.
Rules one day, wild abandon the next.
He will not let go because he can't.

Regret seeps in and fills his hollow heart
with memories of me.

After all the narcissistic girls
calling him five times a day, taking endless
photos, whining, clawing their way into
commitment.

He realises he cannot do better.
And I

could. not. care. less.

Back here

He says that he wants me back
That I'm The One
of course he doesn't use those exact words

he never had much of a way with words anyway
it's been years
He cornered me again

knew where I'd be
Speaking as if we hadn't been apart all those
years – initiated by him

But why would I why should I?
I'm still longing to hear those words
but I just can't anymore

As much as I wanted to see him again
it's agonising being apart *and* together.

Waiting in vain for years for him
to become the man I wanted him to be
need him to be.

After all this time
I see not much has changed with him.

Another delusion of love.

Now I have to fill my heart with distractions
as nothing can satisfy it

        God kind of did temporarily

But it's here again
All I know now is that
I do not want you
back here.

The Second Meeting

We met again this time
he brought my poems

Demanding I tell him which were about him
I have more, I'll never tell

There's this guy I see
a songwriter he wants my poetry as song lyrics.

I wanted to sing them, but they'd
just break my heart.

I decided that a long time ago
my heart is my art.

I know I've paid a huge price for it but it's all I
have and my only way of escape.

I wanted a man to come along
and change my life

but you have to do the work yourself,
alone.

Of course, he gets closure in our meeting. He
gets the last say because it was always all about

him.

I am firm this time. I can't take it anymore.

Leave me alone. Forget I exist.

Just, go.

V Poet's Life

Life of a Poet

Sometimes when I write poems
I eat chocolate truffles
Slowly…

As if it's creamy champagne centre is the only
source of comfort in my life
its sweetness the only goodness lingering.

The night that follows will be sleepless as the
memories of despair
and lovelessness are inflamed.

Insomnia sits upon my bed
like a neglected lover.
Silk pillowcases and sheets envelop me

as I spend another night wishing
you were by my side. As much as all the
tragedies in my life send me to despair,

I know without them I'd never have my art. My
best poems are written by hand on pure white
paper, when I have listened to sad songs, songs

that remind me of you. And sometimes I still
look at the photos of us and wonder what could
have been.

I even listen to the songs you like as if doing so
will fill the room with your presence. Your
absence is a reminder again that I am unloved

and unlovable
it is painful to think about
but that is how I feel.

I know you think about me because I always
think about you. We're connected that way;
we always have been since we met.

There's not a day gone by when I haven't
thought about you. But I'm here, you're there.
Deep down I know

nothing will make you come back. Instead, I
wait for it to pass, be over and eventually it will
be, a day will go by when I've not thought

about you. Though these poems don't help,
instead crystallise, and eternalise my love for
you. My soul speaks through poetry

it pours out unruly during dark nights of the
souls. I strive to keep up with my hand as
I write on cream paper the hurts of the past

and recall yet another lamentable lover. I write
in the early hours of the morning when
insomnia overpowers me and my pillowcase

cannot take anymore tears. It's an endless cycle
agonising but necessary. As I promised my
heart would always be my art.

Other days

Other days I write poetry and look at the
squirrels from my window.

These are good days, blessings, knowing I can
feel myself again and not be weighed down by

all the cruelty life has inflicted on me.
I put on a dress to mark the occasion that I am a

writer, a poet following her passion. Pretty
teacups and home-made cupcakes perch daintily

on my table. John Mayer plays on vinyl. Tears
fall, and I see their droplets upon the paper as

art and remnants of my soul. It is valiant to be
unloved yet love others more deeply.

My suffering is not weakness it is the fire that
purifies my soul and clarifies my view of the

world and the human condition. I read souls; I
echo the deep hurts in all our hearts.

Nobody can hurt me more than my own poetry.
Poetry pierces my heart. But you broke my

heart long ago and now I am wiser and
unmoved by human cruelty.

After all it is so predictable and prevalent
though we need poetry to remind us

that it happens to us all
and we need to remember that no matter what

happens we will always triumph
because we always have.

VI   Back to you

London, Paris, away…

We head back to Paris
after all that is where we met
and your family is here

Searching through Parisian antiques
Galeries Lafayette
Avant-garde designers,
minimalist chic
Parisian streets

We sit for coffee
I thought you were sketching
but you're calculating and perplexed.

And then I meet her
the girl I thought you loved
at the Hotel Plaza Athénée
for Afternoon tea

she is the sweetest sister
and so I confess my first mistaken impression
and we giggle like family.

I can't help but feel that meeting your family is

some sort of consolation.
Of course, I saw it coming…

He is moving to America
it sounds so corporate.

I knew it was too good to last.
The offices are on both sides of the Atlantic so
he will be back every few weeks.
Will an ocean pull us apart?

He didn't get the job in London
instead New York.

He wants me to visit.
Am I tinged with doubts?
Well, I try not to show it. It's amazing,
unbelievable, just like him.

England bound I am
though not for long he hints.
I refuse to move for a man
not my husband.
I am a little upset
though by the time we all go out for dinner
I am absolutely delighted at his news.

Family affair

His mother only stays at the Ritz
I love her already.

Fur coat, black pearls
Paris, London, New York

and LA if her son drags her.
I get swept up by her jewels

but they're good people, honestly
they believe life is about cultivation

that decency trumps all
it's not about what you have

but who you are
it's refreshing.

It took me so long to realise that
Through his relations I escaped the negativity

and it's like I found the family
I always wanted.

Frames

He shipped the art he picked up in
Parisian antique stalls
and sent them to me.

Wanting to know if I liked them.
He liked me to pick frames for the
unloved
paintings
he collected.

Loving you

I fell in love with him
because he saw the beauty
of unloved paintings.

When we were together
he saw the innocence in me
and never tried to hurt me.

It was the way he escaped
the world when he painted.
His endless

sometimes drunken tales of Paris streets,
Maldives beaches and the magic of
Dubai across the night sky.

He was full of stories and poetry
when he looked at me, he said it all.
And when we met

with one look
it had been decided
he was my soulmate.

Letters

We write letters to each other all the time
and share photos. It's so sweet and nostalgic. I
have learned so much about his childhood and

favourite places it's like his letters are black and
white films that come to life in colour as we
speak on the phone.

I appreciate his style, his way with words and
what a gentleman he is. It's like we're in
another era and I like it that way.

My dresses are just as excited as I to see him
and he's always teaching me something new. I
feel at ease with him, he listens as I talk about

books I have read. My reading list is almost as
mountainous as my bookshelves showcasing a
stratum of literary fiction, travel writing and

photography books. He speaks of travelling a
lot of our future and all the places he wants to
take me.

It was his birthday recently and I sketched his
Labrador who I saw faintly in the corner of an
old photo he posted me.

My birthday is not for a while
though he promises we will be together
when the day arrives.

We are apart a lot; I really don't mind as our
world is incessantly connected and the distance
seems to deepen our connection.

My friends say my life has become like a novel
I am not surprised as this is a dream
that has manifested better than I could imagine.

Though often we cannot kiss and hold hands. I
trace my fingers across his handwritten words
and smell the cologne on the paper which he

has immersed onto much like when I spritz my
perfume on his letters. He asked for my
perfume once and I laughed. He said he wanted

to spray it on his pillow so he could feel closer
to me as we are so far apart. I miss him terribly,
but it's the happiest I've ever been.

He says he'll draw me one day. He plays guitar
and I wish he'd write a song about me I've
dropped hints.

I've had many bohemian dreams, some of which are coming to life now.

Secretly I wish to
be immortalised on canvas
remembered in poetry
And to live on forever in a novel.

It was inevitable that I fell in love with an artist.
I had such a habit of falling in love at first sight.
I am often lost in my imagination and wishing

to live life as beautifully as a film. My heart is my art and it's amazing to be with someone who feels the same way.

Some nights I write poetry about him. Though up until now I've been too shy to share them but maybe I will in my next letter.

Peonies on my doorstep

I waited weeks for your return
No call, no text
just agonising wait.

You came back last week
or so I heard.

At last,
I found
Peonies on my doorstep.
With a note for our next date.
Calm returns as I read your sweet message.

Still a part of me looks at your handwriting
searching for clues
as to whether you still love me.

On the day of our date.
I find you
on my doorstep.
I invite you in though purse my lips
as you walk in.

You say you are back now.
That your work,
will let you return to me.

I search your face to see
if your eyes will reflect back another girl.

Although my eyes are brown
they are green with envy.

But I trust you,
because I'm learning to trust again.

Because you are different, better.
Better than what I could have hoped for.
And so, I rid the verdant sin.

And after an hour of your tales stateside I stand
up and walk out of the house a new woman,
renewed from the jealous girl I was.

With you

Loving you is like
a soothing fairy tale
where there are no dragons or witches
hindering our love.

It's simple and dreamlike
I guess it was worth the wait, after all this time
I no longer think or even dare compare you to
the loves before you
because everything is new and fresh and pure.

I outpoured all my heart's hurts
in time for your arrival.

Though I confess I never thought you'd come
that I'd just be a Cinderella at ball
in a manor and not the palace.

I thought I'd missed my chance
but life surprises you, when you least expect it
and dare, I admit it can happen too late in the
journey.

But you're here and I'm in your arms now
and it makes me see how foolish I have been in
the past

Utterly clueless as to what true love was
inevitably as I had endured so much cruelty
that one kind gesture was enough to make me
stay.

When I should have run away
and chased my dreams instead of tolerating my
surroundings and the wicked hearts of those
around me.

But now at long last it has all come together
so I guess it's true what they say
patience, perseverance and wisdom
leads to the right man, the right career, the right
friends, the right path in life

Now every day is like a dream,
and I continue to be an architect
of happier days and wiser decisions
and I get to live it with you.

Fontaine des Mers

Yesterday we were covered in rain
today the sun came out

We are back in Paris again
At the Fontaine des Mers

I have never seen it before and gaze at the
oceanic statues and gold accents

As I look at the water the coins shimmer
like small fishes in the ocean

you tell me to look up
I see the powder blue sky

I'm almost bewildered at why you're asking
me to look up.

I then search around assuming I've missed a
landmark of cultural significance

so I ask you what I should be looking at
You don't reply so,

I look down towards you
And see

                              a Tiffany
                              blue box

I gasp
there is an

emerald cut diamond ring
platinum band with a diamond each side

in the box
in your palm

Again, I look up at the sky, the fountain, the water then into your eyes

I am delighted. These few seconds seems like a lifetime to you

as you are on bended knee
asking me to marry you.

I say yes.
You get up and kiss me

Our lips touch momentarily
we are smiling with joy

My hands stroking your back and arms

I haven't even tried the ring on

You get back on bended knee and put the ring on my finger

A passer-by has been watching us this whole time and offers to take a photo

Our photo sits on both of our phones
and after dinner we share it to all our family.

I'm almost speechless the entire night
and simply smile and look at my ring

Upon returning to England the weight of loneliness has left and I am filled with joy at how beautiful my life has become.

VII Bohemia lives

Princess of Bohemia

A Flower crown upon her tousled hair
Tahitian pearls across her neck

At home silk kimonos lie on the bed
gypsy water on her skin

her hair shines from flower oils.
The scent of her room: the finest perfumes

and essentials oils
In front of the mirror, she stands swanlike

Evenings spent walking along the lake
the swans come out only for her

The tan from Hawaii stays all year
Embellished dresses lay in her wardrobe with

a more exciting life than most
We all know she has been mystifying men.
She lives a Dream life
weekends in the City of Lights

Summers in Hawaii

Winters in St Barts

However, she is no artist, she only embodies the
luxuries of Bohemia; fine wine, good

food, artisanal jewellery, with a curated
selection of men to indulge her every whim.

A Nouveau Bohemian does not make art
instead collects it and hosts soirées,

celebrating the artists who have the talent she
lacks as she spoils them with all they could

never have. She has a terrible habit of falling for
in love with artists and poets.

The spirit of bohemia lives on through her
after all she is paying for everything:

the artist's studio, the theatre productions, jazz
sessions, books, paintings and talent agents.

She is a heartbreaker so never suffers for the art
she tries to create on idle Sundays.

However, her beauty and style inspire. She is an
Artist's muse and men desire to take

photos of her intimately in their studio.
She never lets them of course.

With her background that would be obscene,
and she'd be cut off diminishing her status

among the bohemians. She is breathtakingly
beautiful and desirable yet chooses to live

among the bohemians who appreciate her wit
and mind and money. Other men merely

objectify her, but the creative souls cherish and
charm her. And that is why she stays and

gives up her palatial penthouses and the finer
things in life…

Just for a moment while her starving artist
friends are in town.

Bohemian Royalty

Talitha
Getty Goddess
With a wardrobe that changed the world

From Mojokerto to Rome
she trailblazed fashion
fusing East and West

Bohemian Royalty
wearing Mink fur on her wedding day

Girls with flowers in their hair
and printed Kaftans
Owe much to her

The Unknown icon
leading Bohemian chic
enrapturing generation after generation

The Unsung beauty
with her husband in Marrakech
posing together

Upon a rooftop of a Moroccan palace
a fashion photographer
eternalizes her beauty and style
Moroccan tile backdrop

reposing on silk patterned prints

a gramophone
plays music
channelling psychedelic
sounds of the galaxy

In the fall leaves turn brown
but in her presence
they turn gold and bronze

Her attire a cultural quilt of eclecticism
embroidered with artistry

Heiress of Bohemia
beautiful and damned
bon vivant, possessing what
bohemians desire to acquire
wealth, grandeur and travel

The Untold pain
a tragic beginning, an early ending

Light a candle
Lay white lilies
for her beauty, her pain and splendour
because her bohemian spirit lives on
and reigns in all seeking adventure and delight
in the depths of Morocco, India and Bali

Her life is poetry,
endlessly inspiring
fashion and music
her style woven
into songs and dresses
that she will never know about

She is Bohemian Royalty
And her legacy lives on in girls
Unbeknownst that Talitha Getty sired it all
The Goddess, the Queen, the Duchess of
Bohemia.

Velvet Haze

Bean bags from the tour bus
the guys are crouched down

Girls left the Kensington apartment
Friends not back 'til 4am

I watch him mumble the words Purple Haze
pointing to the wall

I correct him
the wall is cream

He says Clapton. Then lies back on the bean
bag legs tossed in the air.

Reaching for his guitar, he whispers over and
over again Purple Haze, Purple Haze

Fingers swirl and strum in the air
as if orchestrated by a hidden composer

in the wall. The man sees purple
peacocks Magenta tones of iridescence

Eyes fixated on the wall
he collapses.

The next morning Purple Haze is written on the wall. All the song lyrics!

Days later, I write back: Please do not return Mr Hendrix.

VIII   The Loves before you…

Last Summer

They say when you meet
the love of your life
everything changes
you never see life the same way ever again.

On that summer's night their attraction
was immediate.
He played guitar; she wore a cream sundress
Flowers in her hair to hide devilish horns.

She teased him wildly and
he chased her and chased her.
It was too late when he realised
her heart read: danger do not enter.

How could anyone leave such a fragile
creature? When Sundays are filled with charm
and the scent of pancakes in the kitchen
as she serves it to you with ice cream and a
smile that says she has an appetite for other
things.

When she laughs and cries
in the space of an hour…

He didn't.
but she did
And so,
alone in his thoughts
He realised
my pen is my paintbrush
my notebook the canvas.

I will draw you and paint you for the rest of my days…

The Guitar

One day alone in a room
he sat playing his guitar
realising if he couldn't be with her
he could write songs about her.

Lyrics expressing all the words
he wished to say…

Her laughter inspiring melodies.

The longing night after night
created his greatest art,
an award-winning masterpiece.

Now, we all know his name.
But he will never forget hers…

By the Lake

We sat on the grass field.
Picnic. Plaid rug.
You eating fast
looking at me.

I take one small bite.
Because I'm sad and lonely.
You lean in and kiss me.
Impatient, fast.

You unravel my dress
the straps fall...
Nothing guarding me from your selfish grasp...

You unzip and slip
We are one

Tears fall down my face.
You place your hand behind my head
and whisper:
"My beauty, my love don't cry."

You nuzzle your head into my neck
and lean deeper into me
following the scent of your desire.

You tell me you love me.
My heart is so broken
You love me back to life
but it is not enough.

You kiss my lips, my cheeks,
my forehead.
You gaze into my eyes

Hands tenderly slip down
affectionately, considerately…

Again, you whisper:
"I love you."
I don't move.

Tears just fall down my face.

It's too late,
I needed this in an earlier season.
You came back
for no reason.

You ease in and out of my life
as you do with
My Body.

But still, I hold onto you

and whisper for you to
hold me,
love me,
adore me....

Restore me.

IX Passions

The Fall

Secretly we all wish
we could lose ourselves
in someone
drown in love
be overwhelmed in obsession
enveloped in lust
consumed in passion
and lost in hedonism.

Deep / the depths of her soul

This girl is deep,
she's pure poetry
violent with emotion
cunning with insight
a pleasure to touch
and so lonely
she'll do anything for me.

This girl is deep,
she is pure art
violent with passion
with a voracious appetite for sin
and so lonesome
she'll do anything for me.

Ethereal / Ephemeral

She was the girl of his dreams…
Like a cloud, magical to look at
around on inclement days.
Yet agonizingly
unobtainable.

Sometimes you fall in love with someone
not because of who they are
but because of who they remind you of

The relationship is created out of a
Bittersweet longing
for the one you truly wish to be with.

I can only be with you
in your wildest dreams.

My heart belongs to a bohemian.

He collected rare art
read first editions
and only slept with virgins.

Bohemian Love

Anyone can love who they love
marry whoever they desire

which revokes the forbidden of a true bohemian
love as tragedy and anguish are part of

it amidst the passion and magic of it all
amidst the longing of your heart made manifest

its beauty, pain and power lies in the fact that
these two souls so perfect for each other

so deeply in love simply cannot meant to be
together. As much as they hope, wish, long for

and dream there are forces keeping them apart
because together they would never live out their

true destiny as much as bohemian love is
predestined. Love is far simpler, it is the

marrying kind, with the potential for children
and it really is too conventional for a bohemian

soul therefore, only Unfulfilled love is
Bohemian love,

it is that longing, yearning consuming love of a
soul you crave.

Love is eternal and their love is most potent in
memories, photographs and love letters that live

on in songs, poetry, paintings and your heart
forever.

We invoke our lover in dreams and wake up
alone with overpowering endless wishing,

longing and dreaming. The day comes when
you have to drown it out of your soul and

eventually that day arrives and you may even
find someone new who creates a new definition

of love, one less fantastical but steady,
comforting and easier where there is no

heartbreak, parting and sweet sorrow
it will be a love that finally chooses to stay.

X   The sadness we all hide…

Powder room

Standing in front of the mirror
looking back at myself
like a stranger

My perfume whispers:
you have not worn me
since you were last with him.

In defiance I wear the dress
he never let me.

Colour returns to my cheek
as I begin to recognise my reflection.

The scent no longer reminds me of him
after all I chose this scent before I even met
him.

I gaze at photos on my phone
delighted to see that
I am back to my old self.
Standing alone in some,
mingled with others in another.

But best of all is the smile
and allure I take with me wherever I go.

Now that I am free,
I have found myself again.

I cut the ties that bind us.
I threw out everything you gave me
jewellery, silk scarves, not the perfume but the
photos are gone.

Now I know that I am over you.

I see through scent
my perfume imprints
my essence
as I walk into a room
as I get closer to another man.

My ex has dispersed into my past.
Sitting in a small bottle
upon a cabinet.
Alone &
untouched.

Waiting to be smashed
by my pet cat
as she naughtily

climbs upon the cabinet
while I am out at the party.

Coming home,
I cannot feign ignorance or distress
as I see the smashed glass
and overpowering scent.

I sweep it dutifully
as if a ritual of painful goodbyes.
The glass gathers,
and cuts me like a paper cut
refusing defeat.

It has now been swept away.
No longer gathering dust.
And now remnants of you
no longer live in my home.

And now remnants of my love for you
have vanished into thin air.

By and Bye

I dream about you
but I wake up without you.

I'm in love with you
but I can't be with you.

You're always on my mind
but you never have time for me.

I see you but
you don't see me.

I'll always remember what we had
you forget so easily.

All I have are memories of you
that will weigh heavy on my heart forever.

Lonesome

The greatest tragedy
that lay in her heart
was that the one she loved

The First One,
the One

or so she thought…

Well, he was the one
who attempted to enter her
uninvited.

It tore her
left her broken
in two.

So now she remains
alone
solo &
lonesome.

The Notebook on the mantlepiece

Inside the cottage.
Upon the mantlepiece
rests an inherited clock,
cloak of dust and ornaments.
A pinecone sits alone.

After he lit the fire,
we sat on the floor eating supper,
drinking wine. Poinsettias gazed warmly at us
but I could still feel the cold from his body.

I got up and picked up the wool throw
and wrapped it around myself.
He gets up too and walks to the mantlepiece.

I've waited for this moment for so long.

During moments alone in the cottage I have
been so tempted to take a peak.
But it felt like a betrayal
As if I were reading his diary.

Finally, he picks it up
his notebook.
There are drawings of me
page after page

pencil, charcoal
sketches
of my face, body,
positions in bed
as I slept…

His drawings are achingly beautiful.

Months later we broke up,
sometime after that I received
a parcel in the post.

It was his notebook
haunting me.

I kept it on my bookshelf for years and on
lonely winter nights would pick it up and trace
my fingers over the lines he sketched.

How could someone who spent so much time in
love with me just suddenly leave?

When the Winter blues came, I'd open the
cream pages and look at myself.

A solemn rite
I could not let go of.

That November night
I lit the fireplace.

It brought back memories of our last Christmas
together. This time I did not feel hurt or anger.

Just the coldness of the room.

So, at long last I did what
I should have done all those years ago.

I burned your letters, your drawings
and all that I had left of you.

Crown of tears

He gave her the Harry Winston
engagement ring.
The Lorraine Schwartz
earrings.

Her make-up on
hair undone.

Then he uttered those
cold words
in her ear one last time.

He wanted to complete
her look for the night
not with jewels
but with
tears.

Reflection

I tried on her perfume once
then I looked down and found my hand
reaching for her hairbrush
her strands still entwined.

For a moment I was tempted to use it
as if doing so would transform me into her
then I'd know what it was like to be
truly loved by you.

After all she was the only one you
ever loved.

I knew it
deep in my soul.

But of course, I am in denial
because you are so handsome
and such a catch that for some reason
I'll never know
decided to choose me.

But I see her, in the corridors
in the chambers of this manor.
She follows me and in my foolish curiosity
I look through her belongings

trying to decipher why you
would be with me instead of her.

Her belongings hold a greater presence in this
house than I do
I know it and resent it.

Even though
she is dead

She walks so proudly across the estate
admiring the rose gardens every evening.

Every year on the night of your anniversary
she makes an appearance in the
master bedroom
every time I look in the mirror
she looks at me and laughs.

She's there behind me
mocking me
appalled at my tastes
judging the décor.

Even when we are together,
she is an uninvited voyeur as we make love
she whispers to me
as if commanding me

and I listen because
she knows you better than I do
as much as I delight in your sounds,
I know it only arises because
she instructed me to do so.

And so, I cannot take claim you of your
passions the ones I so desperately desire to give.

I am a construct of her
I must be
because you miss her so dreadfully.

Why else would you be with me?
I am malleable and naïve.
I guess that is what appeals to you.
I know I'm being judged and
compared to her.

Every aspect of me is. How can it not be? After
all she was a great beauty who threw
magnificent parties and was adored by many.

I am only barely admired by you.

I bravely walk in front of the mirror and gaze at
my face, I do not see her reflection anymore.

I accept the flaws reflected back at me
and I decide to stop her voice once and for all.

She is livid and all my anxieties
come rushing back.

But I look nothing like you,
our personalities are different.
"No, I am better," she mocks back.

I am not an inferior version of you.
I am me and he loves me for me,
he likes me for me.
You are just jealous because
you are dead, go admit defeat.

"Never!"

I grab the hairbrush and throw it at the mirror.

As the glass cracks, I hear a scream.

And I know at last she is gone.

Now in the reflection I see
myself a hundred-fold.
I see the girl he fell in love with.
The sweet, caring, pure soul he loves.

The door opens. I turn back.

It is him, my love. He has come back to me.

I walk towards you and hug you;
you stroke my back as I lean in.

You are always so loving, giving more affection
every time, we embrace.

I have been a blind fool. Suborned into
inferiority by a ghost of the past.
A person who was just as despised
as she was admired.

In your own words you speak of her
manipulative ploys, how she lied about a
pregnancy and miscarriage. Of her countless
affairs, how she only wanted you for your
money and how much she pretended
her way through life.

And in that room with the smashed looking
glass, we peered into each other's souls,
admitting our faults, misunderstandings, and
fearful experiences of the past.

Hearing all this, hearing this truth gave me such

relief that I cried and smiled at the same time.

And though we were so emotional you told me
to close my eyes and I sensed you
reaching into your pocket.

As I opened my eyes, you presented
a small box.

Let me surprise you again at the party. I've been
waiting, planning I wanted to do it with all our
family there because what's yours is mine and
mine is yours.

And I wanted to make you smile and confirm
my love for you because it is eternal, and I do
mean it when I say I love you.

I cannot believe the undue stress you have been
under. To be perfectly honest I have felt it too.
Being back here, I know this has long belonged
to my family, but I think we should move.

Find a place of our own, together, a fresh start.

I smile and nod in delight and a tear of joy
streams down my face and you gently wipe it
away and kiss me once more.

I have finally awoken from the nightmare and life feels like a dream with you.

A year later and we are married, and you speak of wanting to have your firstborn. You'd like a son but are equally delighted to have a girl as beautiful as her mother, you say.

We have not returned to the house, only for occasional family dinners.

But when I walk back, I feel nothing, I am simply in the present moment ready and happy to make so many memories.

We take photos, and as I gaze back at them, I feel I am looking at someone else's life, but this is mine, all mine, my life, the one I have long deserved and am finally living.

And now finally I get the love I have always wanted returned so abundantly to me from the man I love.

XI   One Dark night with you…

Volition

You went too far that night
I remember after you walked me home
you gave me your hoodie
and I took it as a sign that you cared even
though an hour earlier you violated me.

it was cold and dark

You knew I was a virgin
But you kept forcing and forcing

I froze thinking this was it
this was how I'd lose this moment through your
selfish volition

Yet somehow, I summoned the strength
With both hands I grabbed your most dominant
hand that grasped at the straps
And I managed to pull your hand away

You the Attempted

Put your hand away like a criminal
putting down their gun

I don't know why you stopped

Thankfully, I arrived home still a virgin

I was saving it for you anyway, so why did you have to be so forceful?

And that's what made it so hard to see and feel and know and acknowledge that you tried to rape me.

We were so in love that summer and you were my first everything

Almost.

That's why I couldn't let go and so we simply tried something else that night, but I couldn't complete it as you were not gentle like the last time

And when you walked me home, I was even more on guard

I ended up apologising for not finishing off what you wanted *after* you attacked me

I, the walking victim, with a criminal at her side

And I was in denial for weeks, years really and
then you dumped me, but I never stopped
loving you

I knew what you were or perhaps still are, yet I
still went back to you time and time again
because you were all I had.

You were *and are* all that I have ever had
the closest I came to love and passion.

But you violated me and never acknowledged it
after all the make-ups and break-ups.

Yet it was I that felt guilty.

You never feel anything with your callous soul,
no repentance just self-serving desires

The spectrum of abuse is vast and not
all hatred and cruelty.

I know you still love me and
I still love you

Though I shouldn't

Not after what you did to me

You just seemed like a good guy
though you never were to me
just in my imagination

I love you and miss you, though you broke my heart many times, even now you do it as I see you with another girl.

I wanted to move on
I tried to
but the rest were just fleeting, transient

One was seismic though not meant to be.

I confess that I still love you and cannot hate you
sometimes I forget
maybe I have forgiven you,
forgiven you more than the others.

Maybe I mistake forgetting with forgiving, it's better that way, easier.

I love you like a fool and that's why I must stay away because you are no good for me

I see you have moved on and loved other girls,
getting to be in love, in lust,
in relationships
not that you deserve it

but you're handsome,
so of course you get away with it
You get all the things I wish I could have, like
the love I deserve.

Though I refuse to believe that
destiny will be so cruel.
I will have better, the best guy for me
and he will love and cherish me
the way you did not
but instead do to all the other girls after me.

It does seem cruel that you get to move on, and
experience love and passion and I've just been
alone waiting for love,
waiting to be loved.

But the wait will be worth it, and I will get what
I deserve.

At least that is the lie that I tell myself.

Even if I don't, I'll never let you diminish my

dreams of true love and my longing to at last be
loved in return.

It's all I've ever wanted.

Though really, I always wanted it
to be with you.

I miss you terribly but there's nothing I can do
so every now and then when a blue moon falls,
I write a poem about you, countless poems
about our good times together and how I wish it
could be with us.

Before your dark night of volition.

No doubt a forbidden memory you
indulge in and take pleasure in
that almost ruined my life.

I hate that I love you, but they say love is
eternal, yet nobody tells you that love is not
always returned and can be an emotion so easily
tainted and corrupted and weaponised.

Love can sit as a poison vial in the heart
insatiable awaiting to be awakened
lethal to consume

and with the potential to kill at any moment

Yet we crave it and chase it hoping
to finally get our hearts desires

But love, or rather the path to true love is a
battlefield with Mr Wrongs along the way and
through perseverance and patience you will
encounter

Mr Right.

Armed with this truth I know after all the
struggle and waiting
I will get the love I deserve.

XII   Love Destroys

Maybe love isn't what we think it is

It drives us to despair
binds us to toxicity
a tool for tolerance
of the wrong kind
oh to be kind to them is so wrong

Not to say hate should be
administered
just neutrality
as if they were a stranger
but they are not
they are our lovers,
our mothers, brothers,
colleagues, childhood friends,
hiding under a mask
they hurt us more than criminals

they are criminals of the mind
heartbreak their violence of choice
betrayal their tool of control

the enemy is all around
evil resides in the hearts of these
people we see everyday

Pettiness is the root of all evil.

Any chance to put you down and they'll take it won't they? That is evil. They gleefully reach their hand out with a hammer of attack to destroy you quietly

doing so with a smile.

Unprovoked.

a free pass to hate

perhaps we need to be educated on what love actually is

because it is not like what it is in the movies

love is a verb as the song says

it is patient, kind, loving, persevering

as the bible says:

1 Corinthians 13:4-8

it is an art, a skill, a natural talent though it must be cultivated, deliberate and rationally executed if we are to be true givers/practitioners if it

How many lies betrayals and hurts have been tolerated and defended in the name of love?

Justice must prevail

fairness decency are more important than mere love and compassion as there's nothing more disastrous than false compassion and over extending empathy

w h o   a r e   y o u t o k n o w
h o w   o t h e r s
f e e l a n d t h e i r i n t e n t i o n s ?

How could you possibly know the mind of a sociopath, narcissist or psychopath ?

The worst enemy is the lover
with their charisma,
beautiful or handsome face,
tempting body
engaging mind
that secretly
harbours deceit, rage, revenge and intolerable desires.
And they take it out on you.

And get away with it.

Women
forgive so easily
the crimes of men
and so the cycle continues
of broken hearts which they make broken
homes with

Out of desperation
governed by a biological clock

It only ends when you leave
and by that time so much is on the line

Sadly, once it's over the cycle repeats
as you have birthed one and raised one
just like the man who hurt you and so as a man
they repeat and devour their next victims:
a generational curse of many nations, too
ignorant to pray for deliverance.

Looking out onto the garden

Overnight his garden elegantly dressed itself in
a blanket of snow.

That morning he held his cup of coffee and took
the time to savour it

Working from home he has
late mornings with later nights

Whiskey out of the house
no drinks, no foods left

Christmas was over making way for
New Years

This year it would be different,
it had to be

wishful thinking filled his mind as he sipped
coffee on his out breath he released a prayer for
a better life.

When I Look At Her

When I look at her, I count the ways she is similar to me. I notice her Asiatic eyes, her high cheekbones.

I see every distinguishing factor of my looks in her face.

I am satisfied.

Though I confess I am devastated that you are with someone else. But thankfully she looks like me and that means you've never truly gotten over me...

You search for my face in every girl you see, and I take delight in it. Not that I want you, of course, I just want you to want me forever...

I want you to be haunted by my face, my curves and my essence... Forever.

This way to love/Roadblock to love

I just took it the wrong way
I assumed that / misunderstood the distinction
between unfulfilled love and unrequited love
I internalised it as rejection
that ultimately yet again
I was unloved,
Unlovable.
But it was
Fate,
Destiny
and Life that was to blame.
There were too many forces
keeping us apart.

XIII   Waking up with a broken heart…

I Will Remember You

I will remember you
because I Love You.
I love you more than Life.
If I never knew you
I would not be here.
And for that I will love you
unconditionally,
I wish I didn't sometimes
but it was predestined

After all the fights, the break-ups
the make-ups
The time apart
you remain in My heart
As you make it impossible
for me to move on
because no other guy
compares to you.

Everything I never told you

I love you.
You're The One.
If I had my way I would be with
You right now.
We were meant to be together.
I think about you everyday.
I dream about you then
I wake up and cry
Wandering why you left me...

When he fell to his knees

He cried so I reached my hand to his face
wiped his tears.

He broke down.
Fell to his knees,
looking up at me,
begging and pleading.

My hand raised to my mouth
I tried to fight back the tears.
I couldn't,
it was over.

There was no us,
there never could be.

It was doomed from the start.
I never stopped loving you
we just weren't meant to be.

Fate intervened.
It was not part of God's plan.

So, forget me.

You will find someone new

And one day we will be
strangers forgetting
what we had together.

The Hermès scarf you left me

All I have to remember you by is this
Hermès scarf
you left me.
My comfort, my reminder
that you were even real

and not a figment of my imagination
and deep longings
from countless lonely nights
alone, waiting.

I still wear it when at
my favourite places in Mayfair
the places we went to together

As beautiful as it is
I can't bear putting it on as I sit
at my dressing table

it reminds me of you
and all we had,
and all that I lost.

Pale blue shirt lullaby

I saw a lady
inside an upper end
department store
Long hair
Vardo green dress
and jumper

She picked up the same
man's shirt I reached for

Pale blue
Perfect for him

We both turned around
a mirror behind us

and stared at our reflections

Her face forlorn
mine expressionless

We both tugged at the sleeve of our
jumpers

A tear fell on her cheek

I had one too, but it was from
a raindrop on the way in

I stood still looking at the mirror
watching her
Seeing what she would do next

She walked by quietly

I saw she dropped her scarf
It was cashmere

Holding tightly to it
I noticed my perfume on her scarf

A part of me wanted to keep it
but it was so luxurious
I knew she deserved to have it back

I walked out onto the street
But she was gone
Never to be seen again.

The Waves

When we said goodbye,
I was not waving
but drowning
it was the end

Yet our lives always entwine

Because we like the same things,
know the same people
and of course

we were meant to be together

But never will be

I would die if I ever saw you again
Yet not seeing you is just as hard

Think I'll stay in the waves
lost at sea
lost and found
forever
without you.

Forgive me, forgive me

Forgive me, forgive me
my heart is not my own
I'm sorry I loved you
I'm sorry I met you
Forgive me, forgive me for
I have loved you.
And nothing but destruction
overflowed from the chalice
of my heart.

Forgive me, forgive me
I ruined your life
But I confess I could never
have not met you.

Even if all we did
was send each other to despair
so please I beg you
forgive me, forgive me.

When we met

When we met

you gazed into my soul,
or so I thought.

In the end it was just passion.

Blind passion

You pursued me, and I fell in love.

But then you changed.

Expecting me to entice, enthral and entertain you over and over again.

I became exhausted by you.

So, one day there was nothing left to do but say goodbye.

Loves Trivium

I've had two great loves in my life and they are nothing like each other

Their paths would never cross, they don't even know of each other's existence yet question each on some cosmic level

After all you must have been curious to know who I fell in love with after you as you were convinced, I'd never move on yet I did to a deeper love though one left me more devastated than even you could achieve

And you well maybe you were just as arrogant thinking I'd never even been in love before until I met you

Foolishly assuming all these poems were about you, when really they were about *him*

How desperately I wanted to run away with you to be yours and build a new life and live my dream

But then there was you and I always loved you and finding him was like vengeance that I could

find someone better, and I could believe in love
again and experience it to the fullest

Though that was not meant to be

So sometimes I think you won

And after all the years of searching I am alone
though I have found myself my passion
my purpose my reason to live

And maybe that was the greatest love of all
finally loving the girl in the mirror

With him he'd adore having me by his side and
yes it would have been magical

But with you it was always passionate

So really neither one of you could give me what
I want neither one of you could satisfy me

Secretly I'd love to have you in the daytime
as I live out my dream
and we take on the world together

Then I'd come home to you
spending my nights embraced in passions

no other man has made me feel since.

So maybe there is no Mr Perfect and really does there have to be?

as the depths you satisfied my mind
and the depths that he satisfied my body
have been unparalleled

Or could there be a man that can do both that is out there searching for me…

Part of me hopes that's true and another part of me could not care less because I love who I am and who I have become and men are such a heartache and a headache and I have no time for it as I have to manifest my destiny and be all that I can be and satisfy my curiosity not my body not my heart as they often betray me by my foolish attractions to men who are simply not right for me

Now I can laugh at it all
though it brought me many sleepless nights
and too many tears on silk pillowcases

I practically had to abstain from men as another breakup would simply destroy me but after all this time, I am ready to love again for one last time

And when I meet you, I will be grateful that everything ended before you

I'll be a wiser soul who despite all the disappointments in love continued to have such passion for life and an even deeper love to give you.

The Balcony

He stood across the room.
Our eyes met once more.
Tears filled me
"You came back," I whispered.
He boldly walked towards me…

XIV *Girl in the mirror*

I want to be in love with life, always.

Poetry is the echo
of a lonely heart.

Every face you see
is God's artwork
We are his living sculptures
brought to life by Him
who made us.

Portrait de Femme

I took photos of my bare face
because I needed to know if he
truly liked me
and
loved me
for me

And not
simply
expecting a fantasy

A baby doll with plush lips
and porcelain skin

He needed to see the real me

So he could know what waking up with me
would look like and I wouldn't be like all those
other girls.

Everything I want
is on the other
side of my Art.

I'm an ellipses addict...
Complicated... Sweet... Emotional...
Daring yet fearful.
With a terrible habit
of falling
in love at first sight.

I have this completely romantic notion
in my mind that
I am an artist.
Even though I haven't painted in 3 years
even though I cannot finish drawing
my self-portrait.
I still feel like one

maybe I am an artist of words:
my pen is the paintbrush
my notebook the canvas
and you are my muse.

I knew that if I could
imprint my essence into pages,
unleash my soul into books
and speak with my heart
I could change the world.

XV Inside the lives of beautiful people

Sweet Clover

Her hair
the colour of chocolate truffles
on a Sunday afternoon

Her lips
parted gently like a girl in
Wonderland

She is 18. A Virgin.
Her heart as pure as her body.

Delicate frame, dainty features.
Draped in dresses as if every day was
a tea party.

Sweet, sincere
The model of a femininity
Long gone
Lost by feminism

Impearled with her grandmother's wisdom.
She waits for a Gentleman to sweep her off her
feet.

Her Wedding Day will be magnificent
all that little girls dream of
Only her betrothed has yet to arrive.

Little Miss Envied

Wonderland wardrobe
Jewel tones in the Summer
Berets for Fall
Bejewelled necklines for Winter

Porcelain skin
Hair curls at delight

Home comforts:
Mayfair
The Upper East Side

Obscene wealth becomes her.
Enemies attack, she retreats.

Leaves England. Faces New York.
Alone. Suitors follow her.

Choosing men like a sommelier.
Playing them serenely like a harpist.
Only the finest will do as she begrudgingly sees
them on a special friendship basis.

The rise is meteoric.
Elevation: elusive, exclusive and elegant.
No whispers, no compass and unlike many

before her no fingertips leave their trace.

She is enigmatic. An intriguing soul, dazzling
them all this side of the Atlantic.
Onboard Wonderland, where dreams manifest
like mergers and acquisitions.

Woven girl in denim pinafore.

Paint stains on nails
Jam jars with art supplies and snacks. Organic.
Gluten-free.
Handbags, raiment:
prospective canvases
waiting to be painted on

Hokusai and pink cherry blossoms
painted on the walls
the result of ennui

Bare faced. Essential oils. Natural homemade skincare.

Watched over by mother-in-law's tongue.

Collecting succulents and pots. Simple pots.
White pots. Porcelain. An obsession

Handmade, home-made. Made with Love.
Given with expectation.

A manic pixie dream girl.
Waiting for The One.

Parisian fringe, Bretton stripes, denim pinafore

dresses.

A little pup, tugging at shoes as residents enter the house.

In the kitchen
Ceremonial matcha tea set
Hidden as if sacred. Poured as if ritual.

Pots of beeswax, cocoa butter, sea salt

Her favourite essential oils? Can you guess?

With diffusers in each room, you'd be forgiven for not knowing. Rose, lime, black pepper. Where has the scent originated from?

Rosy. Peppery. Sweet and warm.

Neroli. Lemon.

A moment of calm

Mugs line her desk. Draws filled with pens of every type, pencils, sketchbooks and endless scraps of paper with to-do-lists that never get done.

Her life is creative chaos.

She sees the beauty of lateness
the charm of procrastination
and captures the unrelenting urges of laziness
as capsules of self-care.

She is bold, fearless, a free-spirit
as you'd imagine
but she orchestrates the chaos in her life
as it is a life force, an energy-field from which
stems her uniqueness

Making her unforgettable and quietly admired
under all the sighs and frowns.

To walk through life without worry,
To walk through life without blame,
To walk through life like a hurricane

with quirks as debris
wild abandon as destruction
patches of eccentricity sewn into her soul

She is a patchwork of oddities
unconventionally beautiful
quietly intriguing

a unique standing out in a
sea of conformists.

My Valentine

Red roses sit upon Valentina's night table
if they are wilted it means
she and Felipe have broken up
when they are in bloom
they are back together in their
velvet lovers haze…

Inside her wardrobe lay
a collection of silk dresses
one coloured as dark as wine
on winter nights
some are creamier tones and others are
swathes of fiery passionate shades that
sit and lie and fall apart
in her wardrobe.

Her bedroom a boudoir of passions
there are chocolate boxes, candles
silk bed sheets and diaries on shelves that have
her tears imprinted in the ink.

Theirs is a love to inspire countless songs

a lyrical love

Much of Valentina's recent diary entries are

about Felipe. They have broken up and made-up countless times. Theirs is a love that is addictive, intense, few can maintain such levels of passion and despair

Felipe has been with many women, but he always comes running back to Valentina
they are fiery stubborn souls
their words to each other pierce their hearts
but their love is too sensual and tender to sacrifice
He knows there is no other woman like her
and nobody pleases him like she does

But he has cheated
confessing he loves women too much
The only way to finish their
relationship for good
is if she cheats

But she can't because she loves him too much and no man can ever give her that exhilarating rush that he inflicts so artfully on her mind and body.

And so, they are entwined in their
love hate passion

it's been that way for years…
A flame that never dies.

Emerald eyes, Gypsy heart

the sun shimmers on her skin
the moon resides in her soul

There's never an ink of doubt in her.
she was born to be beautiful and have men gaze
at her and she freely indulges it

she loves life

                        she loves herself

debauched in self

obsessed with her reflection

amour propre

but no ego,

just frivolity and passion for life

she is vibrant, beautiful and captivating
            when you are with her you feel
limitless

                  as if part of secret club

                  a desirable inner
circle

Inside her phone…

An archive of breath-taking self-portraits.
Scenes from Mexico, the Maldives and
Morocco.

She has seen it all and will charm you with
stories of her travels

Her gypsy heart needs to wander and explore
new terrain

On the beach she is in her element
free with the water
breathing melodically with the waves

She lays on her beach towel at peace
at one with the universe.

She is beauty manifest
glowing skin
and a smattering of freckles

Her Emerald eyes speak to you as you
gaze at her photos

Photos of her that were stolen
her profile is often set to private

In restaurants waiters line up to serve her

She'll stay all night awaiting a
desert not on the menu.

she is comfortable in her skin
self-care is as natural as breathing to her

she is indulgent, confident and liberated
she cares she shares she worships
herself

no guy could ever cross her and even if he did

she is already onto the next

guy, project, mantra, phase, list, dream,
experience, ambition, passion, enterprise,
venture and affair

I know you're dying to meet her

if you're a girl you'll find her on the King's
Road

If you're a guy the best restaurant to take her to
is Ziani's

Though there's nothing quite as excruciating as
the day she becomes bored of you

One day she will be

You'll sense it.
her cool exterior commanding you stay away,
you did not make the cut,
you are not to exist in her presence.

Many will know her, but few make it into the
inner circle.

She is a contradiction in terms
free-spirited yet snobbish
sexually liberated yet selective

You know you'll never meet a girl like her
and like many before you

know that you are unworthy to be in her presence.

Yet you long to be her, to be with her.

The envy never turns to malice just deep admiration and longing.

Because she loves herself and we would all love to feel how she feels about herself.

She is svelte but has stretch marks,
a hint of cellulite, a few scars, freckles

but none of that can be seen because she glows in her spirit
and radiates the joy of living

And if you get near enough, you too can feel the same.

Prince Albero

Now him and his art college friends are taking private jets out to Miami
Art basel, clubs, Palm beach, Palm spring

The Breakers
If he owned hotels, he'd run a bespoke chain of Heartbreak hotels
Playing nothing but Elvis.
Drinking Jack Daniels under the table.

Lost boy, spoilt man.
Sotheby's, Christie's nothing but the best for our pampered Prince.

His bank: a dry Gin.
Ginnie that is,
Virginia Arvington.

Old money with plenty to waste.

But he's beautiful, green eyed

Tousled dark hair, he knows how to make you feel beautiful with one look and he knows how to make any girl submit to his will.

Yet he stays with her.

He flirts, seduces with words, poetry and sweet nothings filled with expectancy, devoid of truth a luxury of lies fill his mouth and you are forever attracted to him.

As soon as you meet him, you are captivated.
There is so much to him.
Yet he is cold and charming
passionate yet infuriatingly pedantic.
A perfectionist. An Erudite.

Inveigle. Eagle eyes. Loves money more than Mariam. Though we'll never know if they were twin souls.

He has never had his heart broken.

So many girls have tried to capture it
and failed.

But soon, very soon he will meet his match.

A soul more mesmerizing than he
will capture him.
And he will realize we are all
Powerless in the face of True Love.

The Poet

The one who was poetic and athletic
The Dreamy guy
The one you wished for.
The one you waited for.

Then one day...
He walks into your life
and you're never the same.

You wanted a guy with depth and passion.
But his soul runs deeper than the abyss and it's
too much to handle.

Sometimes it's a good too much.
too many kisses, cuddles, adoration
near worship.

He's public with your love, he loves you
unconditionally.

It's too good to be true.

He stands by you all this time.

You fall into slumber.

You wake up thinking now is the day he will leave
Yet he stays.

Because he wants to.

It's effortless, a dream come true.
But something is plaguing him.
It's too late by the time he tells you.

You're distraught. It's nothing to do with you.
It's all him, his past, the darkness.
The abyss, it's overwhelming, overpowering.

The only force that could tear you apart is invisible.

It has no intentions just darkness and fear.

But you'll work through it together,
you want to, you have to.

Suddenly infidelity seems juvenile.

So easy compared to these dark traumas
that plague the quiet soldiers

Men fighting invisible battles for years.

Fighting, hiding.

The Valiant hidden in plain sight.

Scandal. abuse. We all know about it
but never speak it.

You love him even more for saying it.

You cannot believe how beautiful his soul is.
He truly is a knight in shining armour.

A quiet hero not just in your eyes but to all
those little boys kept home crying, staying
silent.

It all unfolds years later, in rage, agony.
Sometime suicide.

But this man will not fall into the abyss,
This dark cloud that captures so many men
And steals their lives will not take him.

As you fight back the tears triggered by this
revelation, you start to have faith in man again.

After all, if this soul can go through all that
and come out as the gentleman that he is
then the human spirit truly is greater
than all the evils inflicted in this world.

And now you can walk in conviction
after hearing this truth because you know that
Love triumphs over everything.

XVI Little tears

Do not hide the sadness
because it will outpour
when you least expect it.

How do you rebuild a life
after you've lost your destiny?

Where there is tragedy
there is art.

I was watching them from afar
and it was so sad
because they were so
perfect for each other
yet could not
be together.

I knew one day I would
fall in love
at first sight

It was with you
It was immediate

though not meant to be.

She loves you more than life.

They parted ways
and spent their days
secretly in love with each other.

I did not realise you were
kissing me
goodbye.

We met to keep each other alive.

Learn to love loneliness
because it's as lonely
as you.

"But you're beautiful,
you can't complain."

You may have a broken heart
but I have a broken life
because of you.

I have only ever been
intimate with sadness

I have only been in a
relationship with loneliness

I have only ever been in love with you.

I searched for your soul
and you filled my void.

"Your soul is a river to my heart."

In one moment, you became my everything.

I loved him and loved him
and he never loved me.

It's agony watching someone
you love
be in love
with someone else.

When you're with the wrong guy perfection isn't good enough.

"Can you just forget me?"
"Never."

I have everything…
But you.

My love for you died
sudden and quick
just like the way

I fell in love with you.

The sudden break-up
felt like an act of
emotional violence.

Heartbreak,
an act of violence
his weapon of choice.

Sleeping on a bed of blood
drowning in a bath of tears.

You thought the world of him,
and he thought nothing of you.

There was a time when
the hope of you
was all I had.

All I ever wanted was to be
young and in love.

Unfulfilled love is painful.

What do you do
when
true love
does
not
return?

I still believe in Cinderella moments…

The End

Once upon a Wonderland

I want to show you this place
come inside.

A bookshop?
Yes, a simple bookshop

Where a fairy-tale unfolded on an Autumn afternoon.

No greater romantic encounter
could be written in the books on the shelf

A New York Times bestselling author was warming
the crowd at his event.

There were droves of people:
literary folk, journalists and beautiful people

Some dressed like it was summer
others in autumnal apparel

Our Prince from Europe was handsome though had no
armour on just a tailored coat.

Our Princess was beautiful and ready to be swept off her feet.

She wore a white sun dress

Her hair long, dark and tousled like mine.

He stands on one side of the room.

She walks towards him
Yet has not noticed the Prince.

Sadly, someone comes over and speaks to her, distracts her.

She keeps it brief
and looks around the room.

Our Prince has been looking at her this whole time…

Captivated

He prays she looks his way.

His wish is granted.

Their eyes meet
they are speechless….
Already in love.

Finally, he musters up the courage and
walks to her, speaks to her,
she smiles…

And that is how their love story began
in this bookshop, this humble abode where
the greatest love story not yet written
was finally told.

It was a love that was
supposed to change the world.
Now they are a
pair of lost souls
apart,
hopelessly in love with each other.

                                        Forever.

***

Look out for Catherine's next book of Love Poems

Lovers in Paris

Please review this book on Amazon!

www.CatherineVaughan.com

Also by Catherine Vaughan

The Quarter Life Crisis Poet

Welcome to Wonderland

www.ingramcontent.com/pod-product-compliance
Lightning Source LLC
Chambersburg PA
CBHW031442040426
42444CB00007B/938